easy piano

mileycyrus

breakout

9	Breakout
14	7 Things
20	The Driveway
26	Girls Just Want to Have Fun
30	Full Circle
36	Fly on the Wall
40	Bottom of the Ocean
45	Wake Up America
50	These Four Walls
54	Simple Song
60	Goodbye
67	See You Again

Photography by Sheryl Nields

ISBN 978-1-4234-6658-1

SEVEN SUMMITS MUSIC

DISTRIBUTED BY

HAL•LEONARD®
CORPORATION

7777 W. BLUEMOUND RD. P.O. BOX 13819 MILWAUKEE, WI 53213

Visit Hal Leonard Online at
www.halleonard.com

BREAKOUT

Words and Music by TED BRUNER,
TREY VITTETOE and GINA SCHOCK

Fast Rock

Ev - 'ry week's the _____ same; _____ stuck in

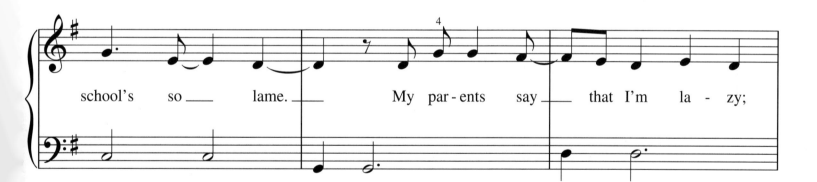

school's so _____ lame. _____ My par - ents say _____ that I'm la - zy;

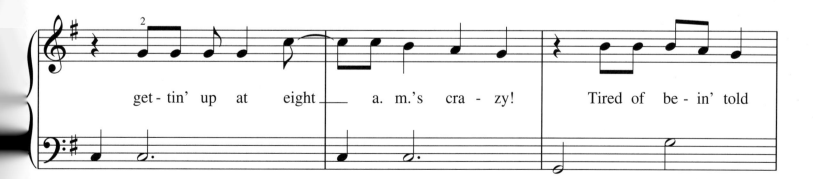

get - tin' up at eight _____ a. m.'s cra - zy! Tired of be - in' told

what to do; ___ so un - fair, ___ so un - cool. _

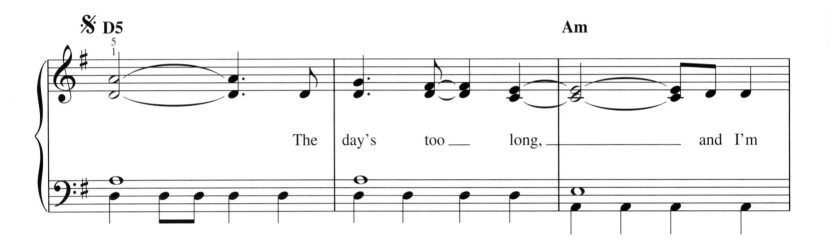

The day's too ___ long, _____ ___ and I'm

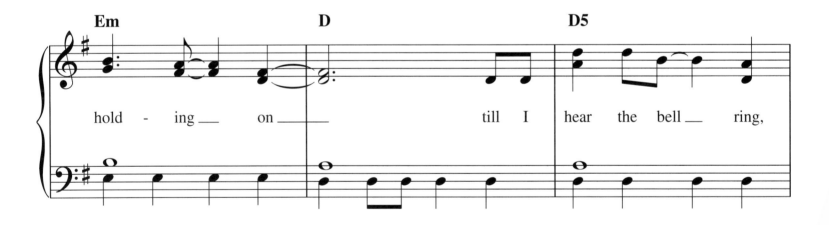

hold - ing ___ on ___ _____ till I hear the bell ___ ring,

'cause that's the time when _ we're gon - na, time when _ we're gon - na

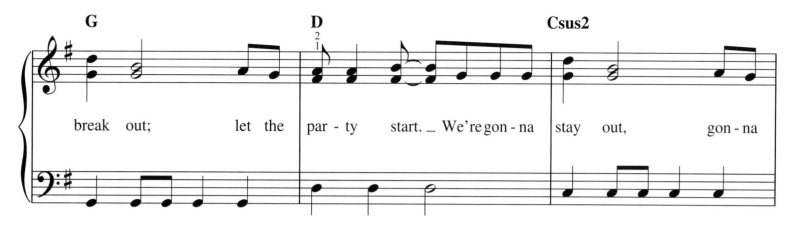

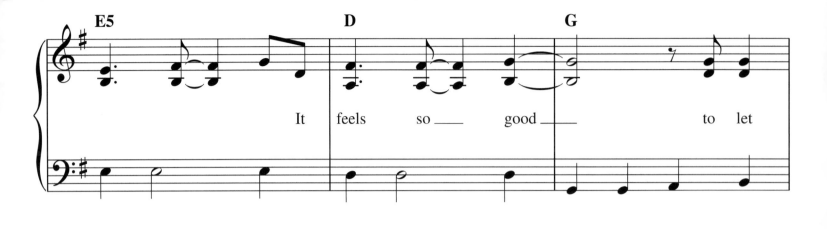

It feels so good to let

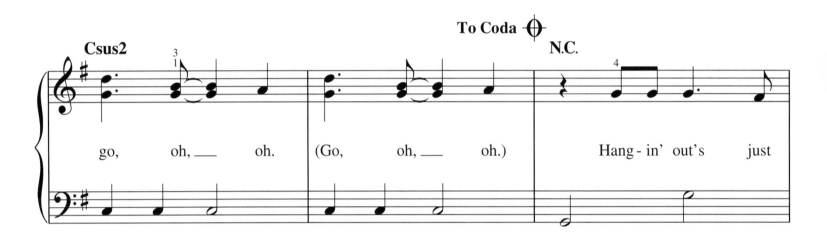

To Coda

go, oh, oh. (Go, oh, oh.) Hang - in' out's just

something we like to do; my friends and the mess we get in - to.

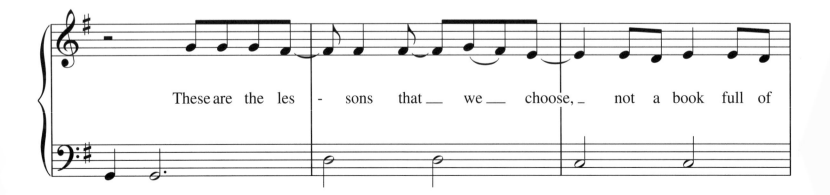

These are the les - sons that we choose, not a book full of

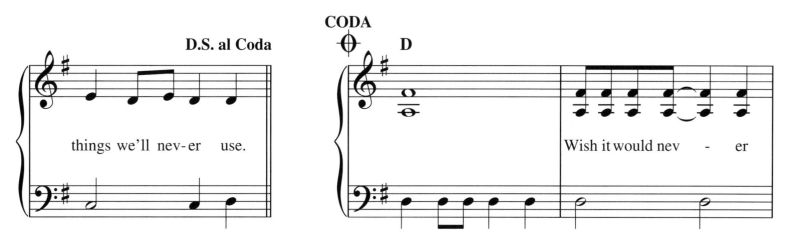

things we'll nev-er use.

Wish it would nev - er

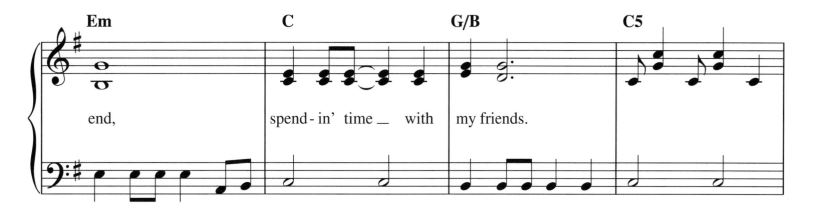

end,

spend-in' time __ with my friends.

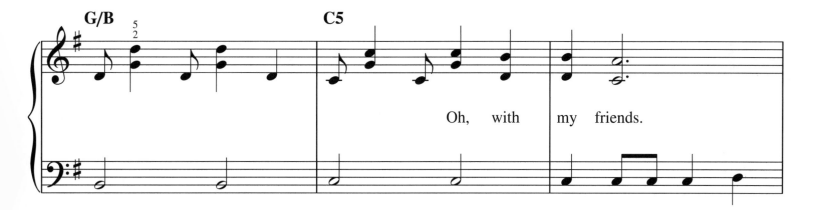

Oh, with my friends.

7 THINGS

Words and Music by MILEY RAY CYRUS,
TIM JAMES and ANTONINA ARMATO

Moderate Rock

With pedal

pro - b'ly should-n't say this, __ but at times I get so scared __ when I
(See additional lyrics)

think a - bout the pre - vi - ous __ re - la - tion - ship we shared. __ It was

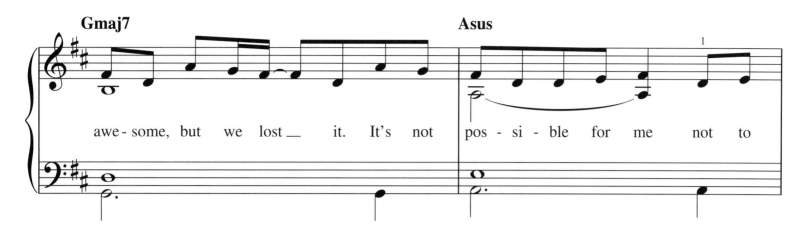

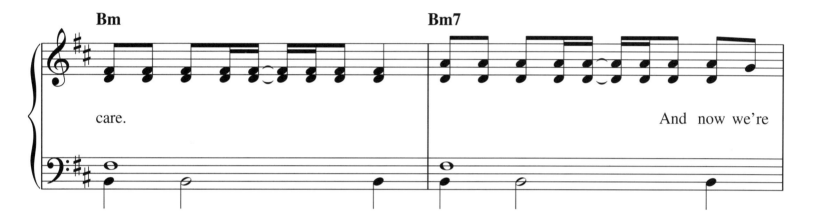

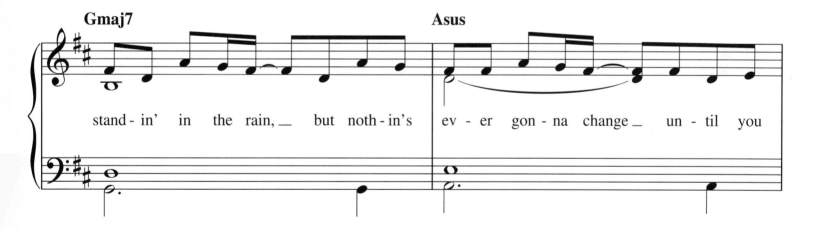

16

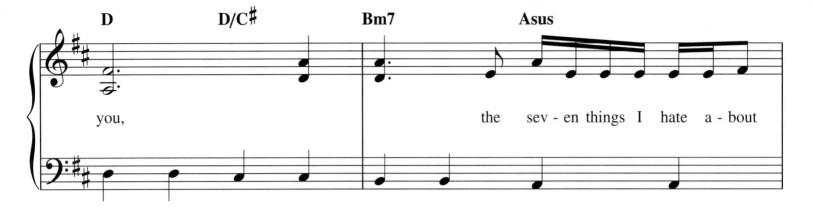

you,   the   sev - en things I   hate   a - bout

you,   oh _____ you.

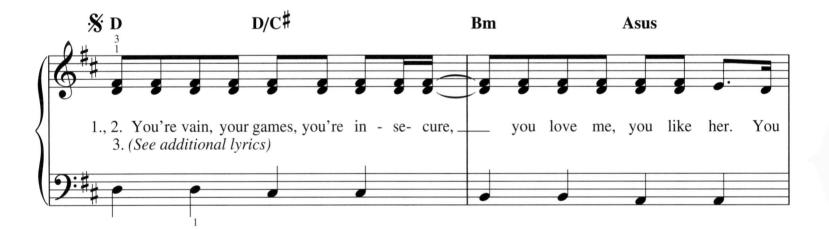

1., 2. You're vain, your games, you're in - se- cure, ___ you love me, you like her. You
3. *(See additional lyrics)*

make   me   laugh, you   make   me   cry,   I   don't know which   side   to   buy.

Your friends, they're jerks. When you act like them, just know it hurts. _ I

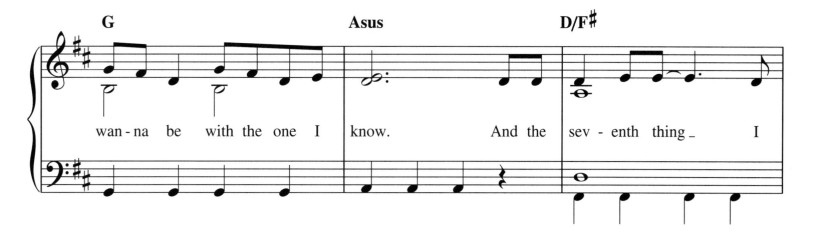

wan - na be with the one I know. And the sev - enth thing _ I

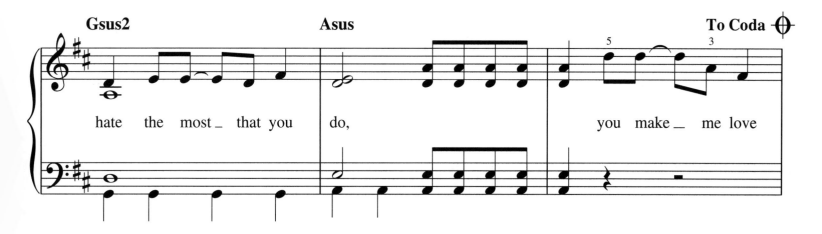

hate the most _ that you do, you make _ me love

you. It's

you.   And com-

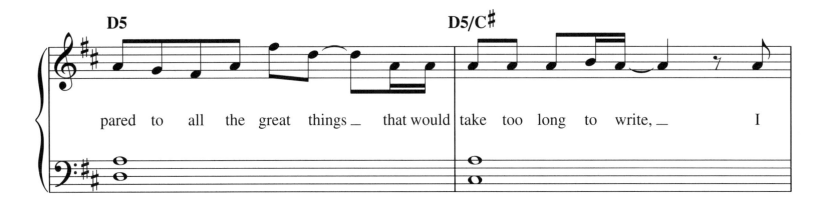

pared to   all   the   great   things — that would take   too   long   to   write, —   I

prob-a-bly should men-tion   the | sev-en that I   like. ——— ——— The sev-en things I like a-bout

you. ———   You do. ———

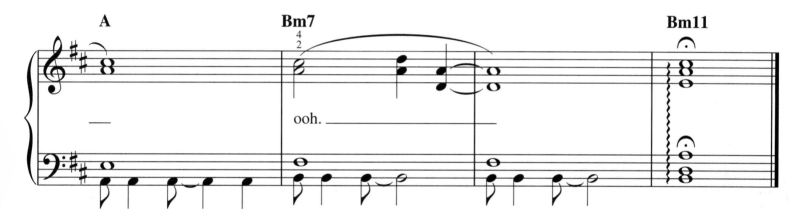

Additional Lyrics

It's awkward and it's silent as I wait for you to say
What I need to hear now, your sincere apology.
When you mean it, I'll believe it.
If you text it, I'll delete it.
Let's be clear, oh, I'm not comin' back.
You're taking seven steps here.
The seven things I hate about you:

The seven things I like about you:
Your hair, your eyes, your old Levi's.
When we kiss, I'm hypnotized.
You make me laugh, you make me cry,
But I guess that's both I'll have to buy.
Your hand in mine when we're intertwined,
ev'rything's alright. I wanna be with the one I know.
And the seventh thing I like the most that you do,
You make me love you, you do.

THE DRIVEWAY

Words and Music by MILEY RAY CYRUS,
SCOTT CUTLER and ANNE PREVEN

21

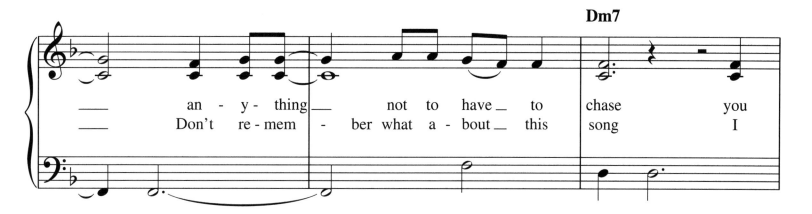

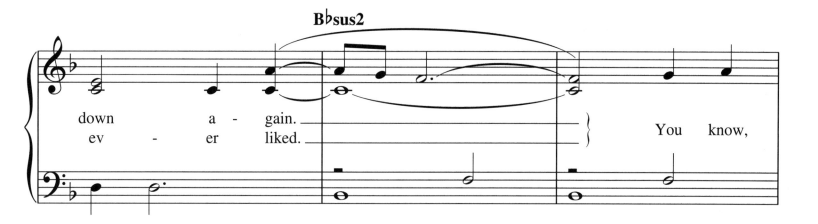

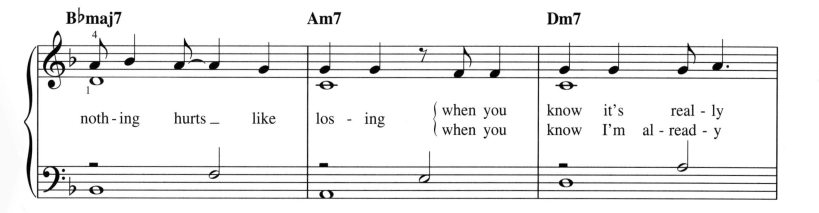

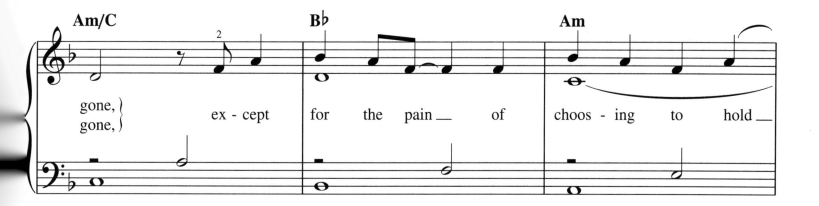

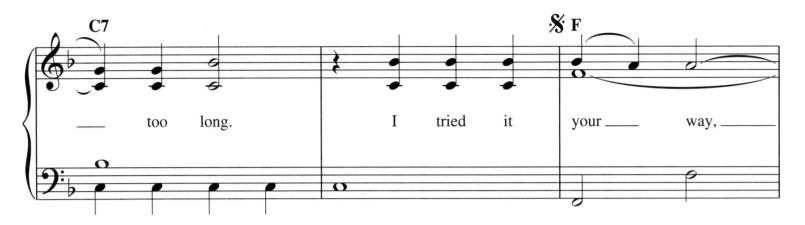

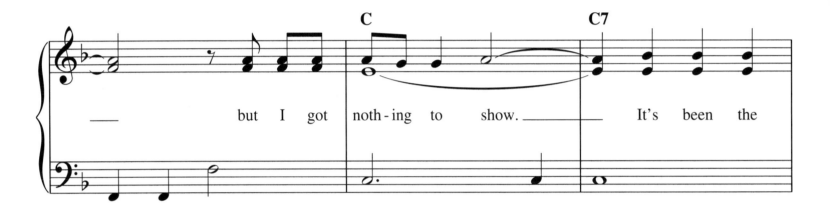

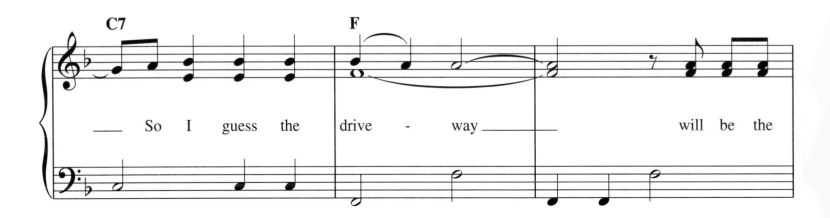

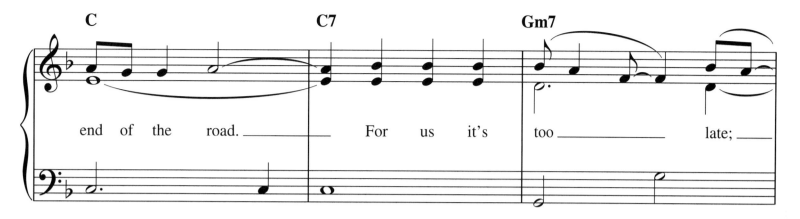

end of the road. ____ For us it's too ____ late; ____

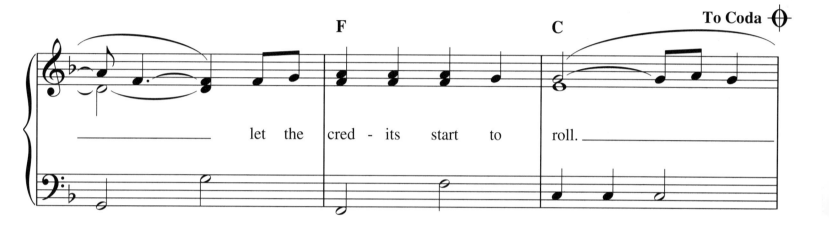

To Coda ⊕

____ let the cred - its start to roll. ____

1.

2.

____ I thought may-be we were get - ting ___ some - where, ___

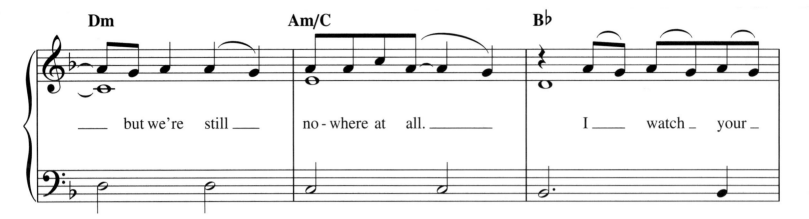

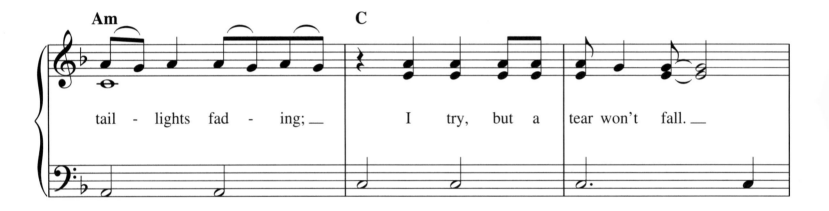

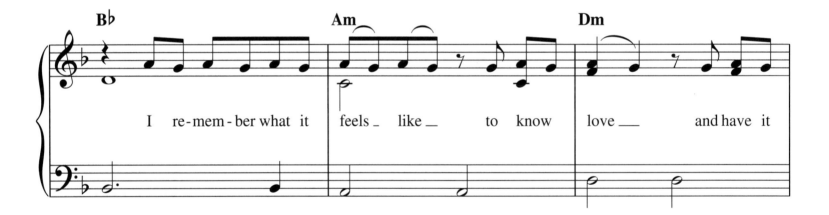

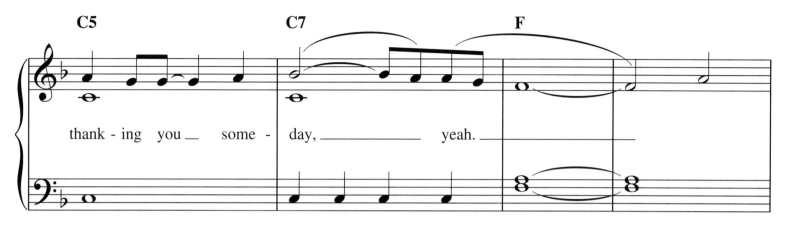

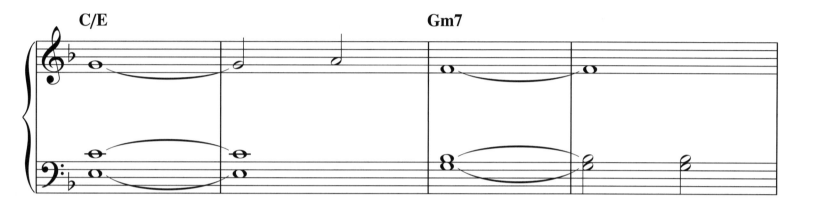

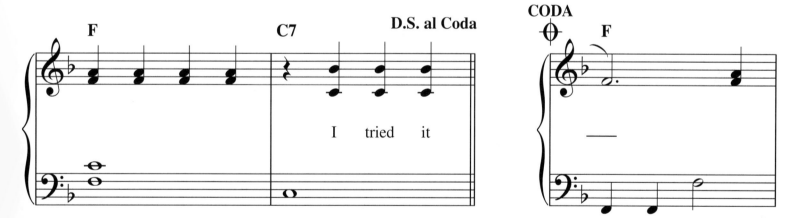

GIRLS JUST WANT TO HAVE FUN

Words and Music by
ROBERT HAZARD

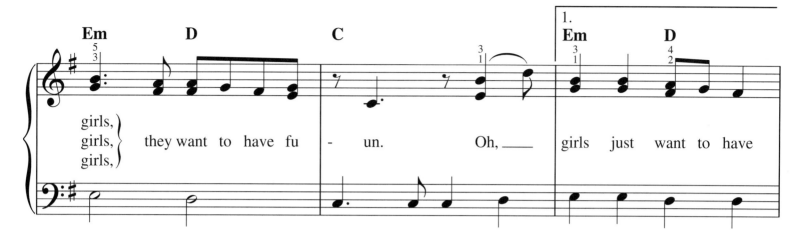

girls,
girls, they want to have fu - un. Oh, ____ girls just want to have
girls,

fun. ____

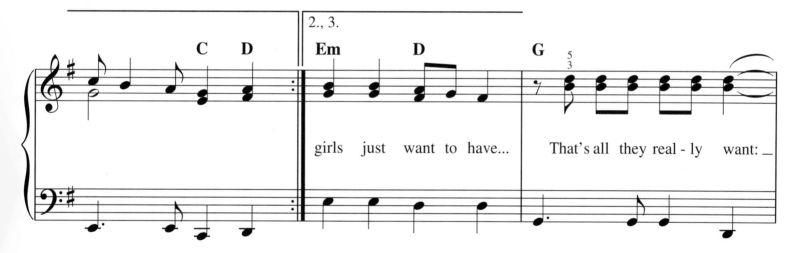

girls just want to have... That's all they real - ly want: _

____ some fun. ____

When the work - ing day is done, _ oh, girls, they want to have fu -

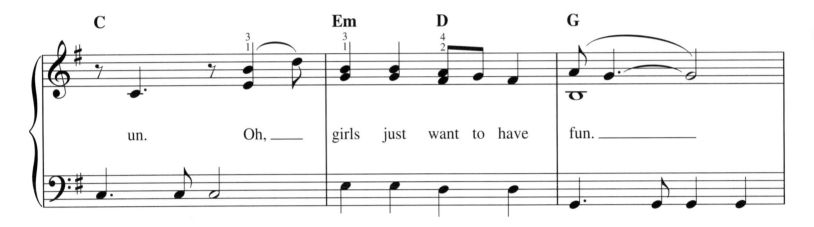

un. Oh, _____ girls just want to have fun. _____

D.S. al Coda
(take 2nd ending)

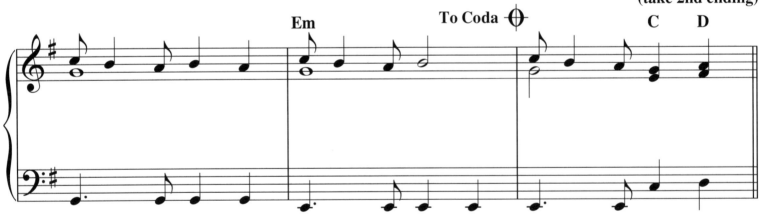

To Coda ⊕

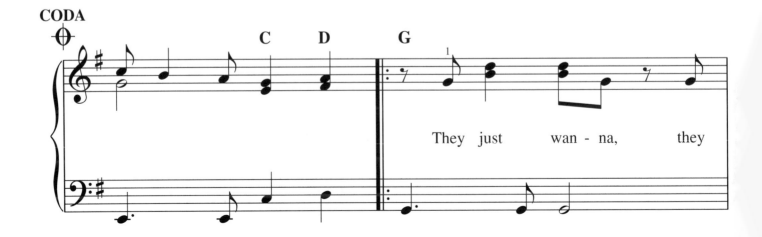

CODA
⊕

They just wan - na, they

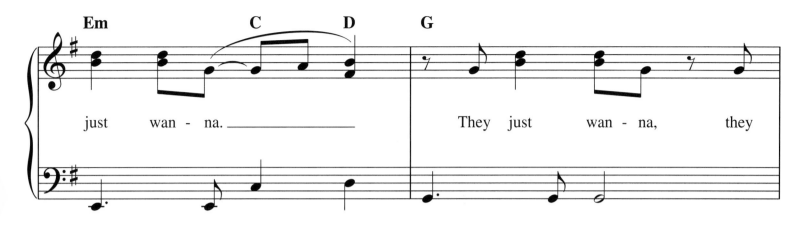

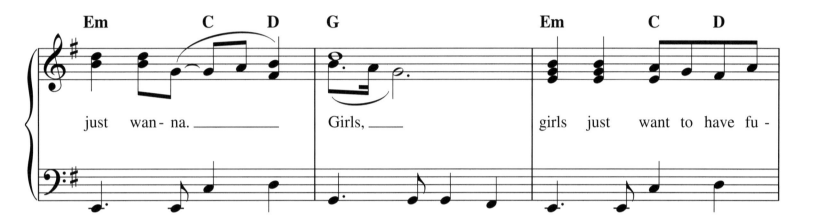

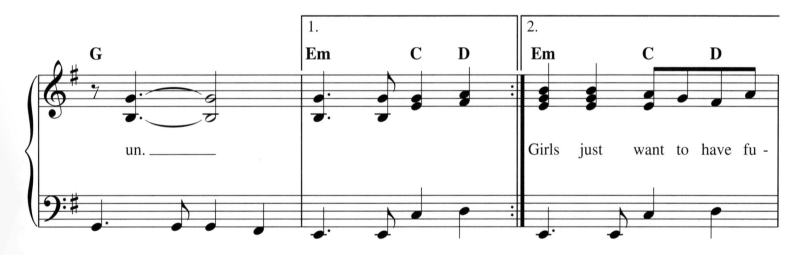

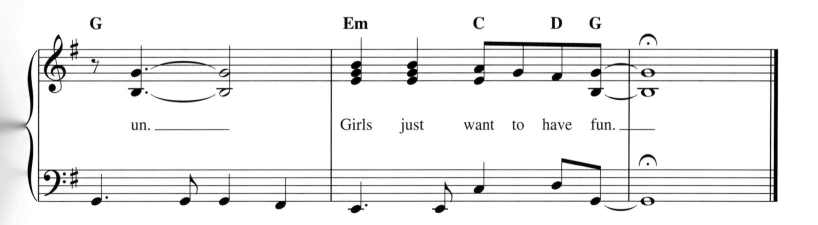

FULL CIRCLE

Words and Music by MILEY RAY CYRUS,
SCOTT CUTLER and ANNE PREVEN

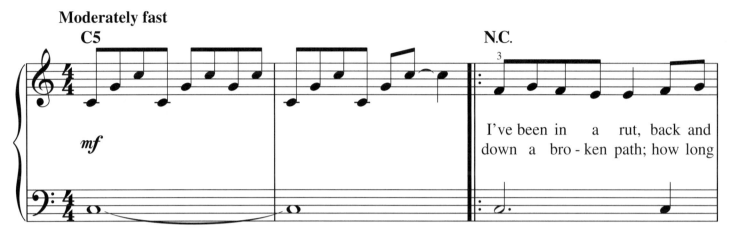

Moderately fast

I've been in a rut, back and
down a bro - ken path; how long

forth e - nough, heart like a wheel. _____
can it last? Please let me know, _____

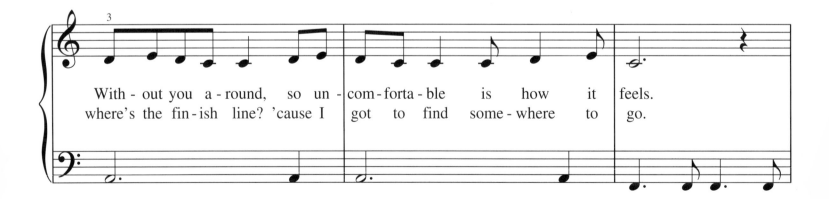

With - out you a - round, so un - com - for - ta - ble is how it feels.
where's the fin - ish line? 'cause I got to find some - where to go.

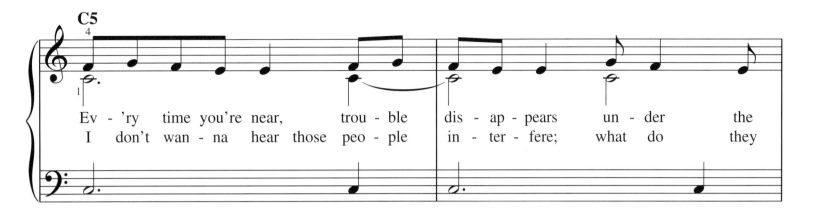

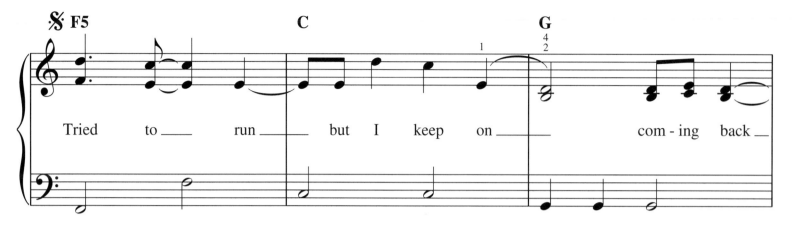

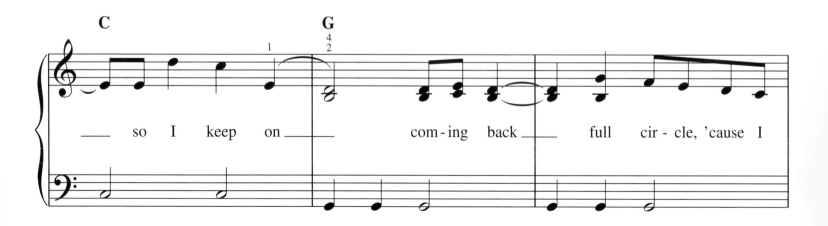

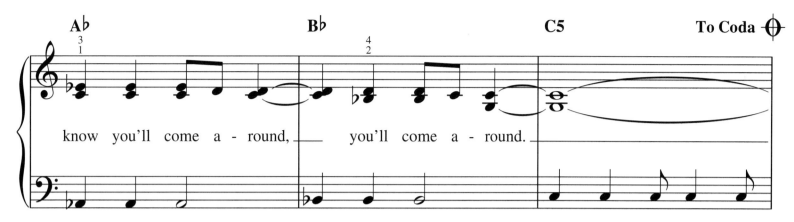

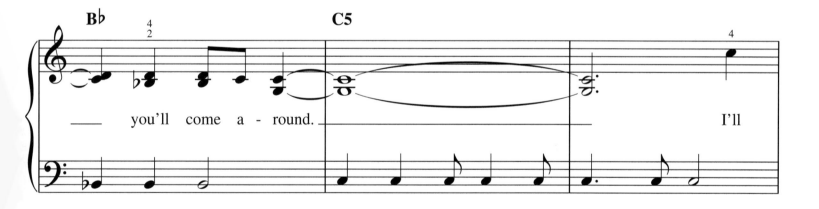

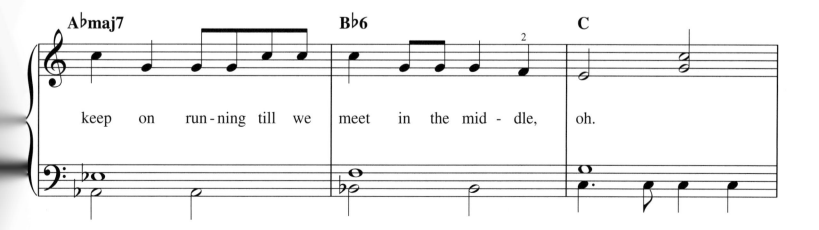

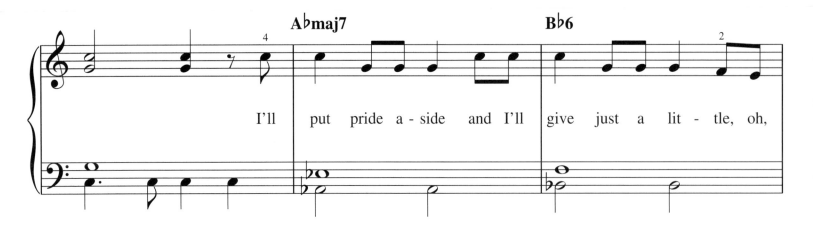

I'll put pride a-side and I'll give just a lit-tle, oh,

oh. _____ There's miles to go, but

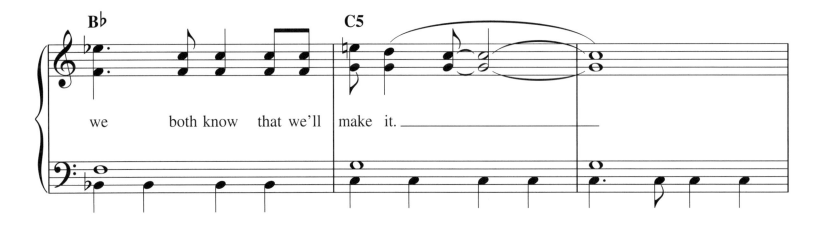

we both know that we'll make it. _____

And I know why. _____

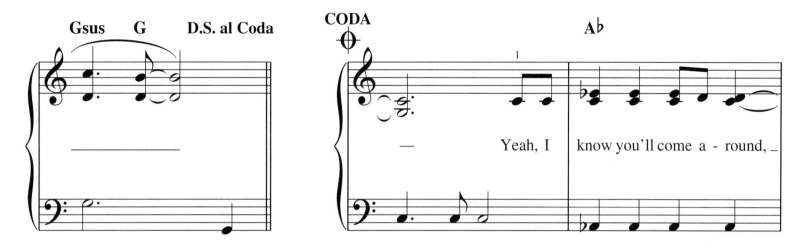

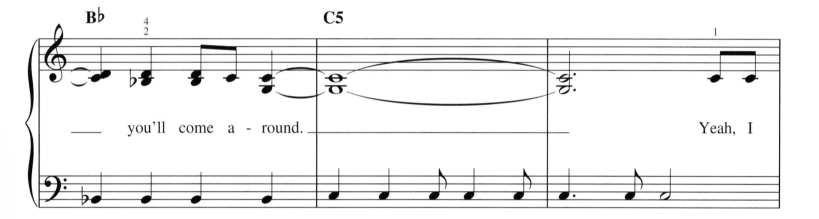

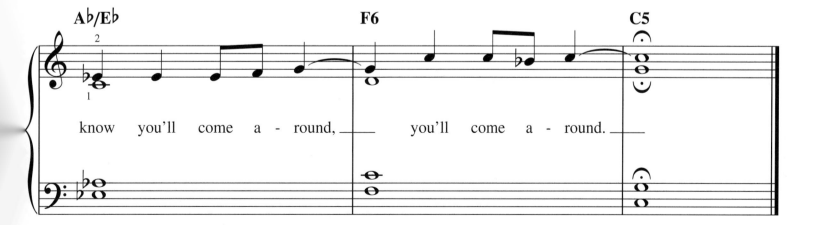

FLY ON THE WALL

Words and Music by MILEY RAY CYRUS,
TIM JAMES, ANTONINA ARMATO
and DEVRIM KARAOGLU

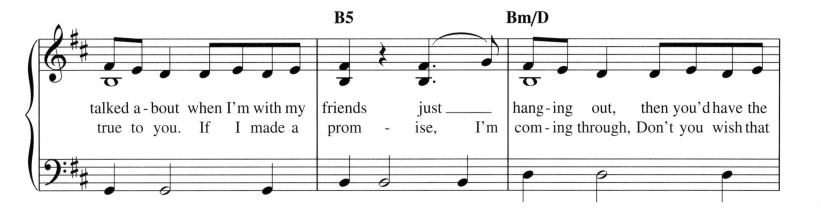

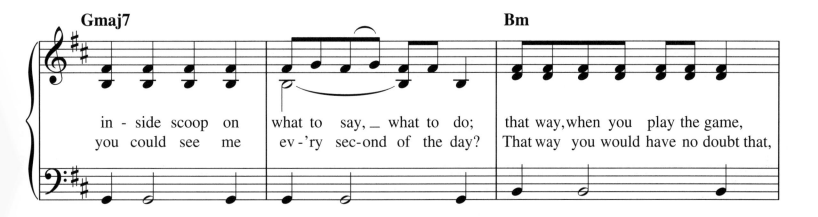

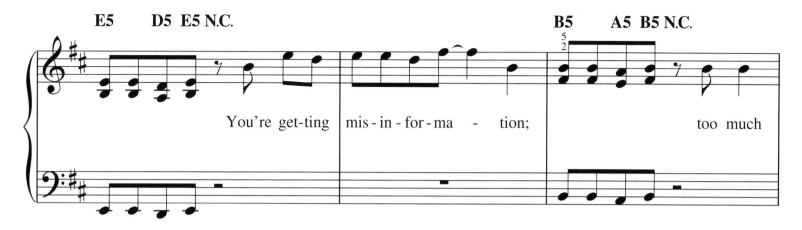

You're get-ting mis-in-for-ma - tion; too much

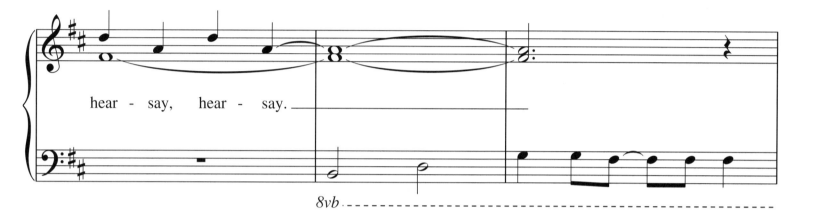

hear - say, hear - say.

8vb

(8vb)

D.S. al Coda

Hey!

(8vb)

CODA

(fly on the wall.)

(8vb)

BOTTOM OF THE OCEAN

Words and Music by MILEY RAY CYRUS,
TIM JAMES and ANTONINA ARMATO

Moderately slow

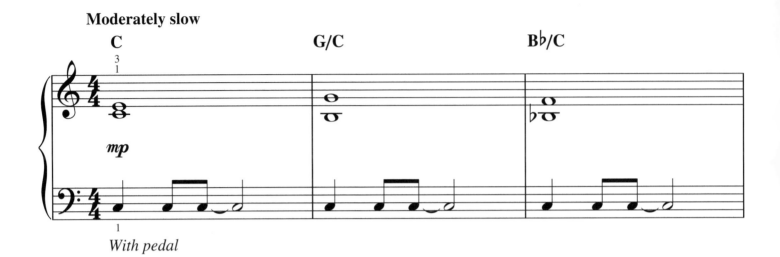

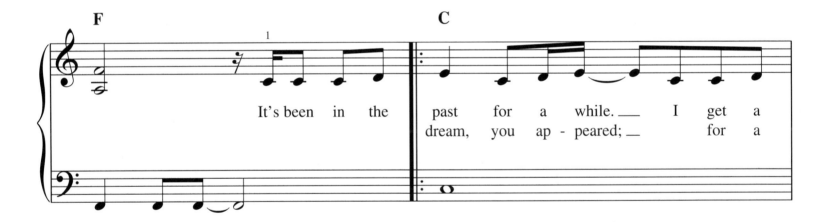

It's been in the past for a while. ___ I get a
dream, you ap - peared; ___ for a

flash, and I smile. ___ Am I cra - zy? Still miss you,
while, you were here. ___ So I keep sleep - ing just to keep you

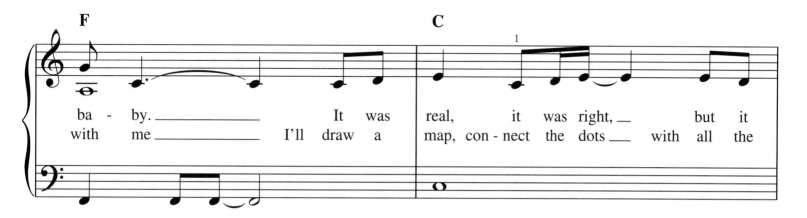

ba - by. _____ It was real, it was right, __ but it
with me _____ I'll draw a map, con - nect the dots __ with all the

burned too hot to sur - vive. __ All that's left is _____ all these
mem - 'ries that I got. __ What I'm miss - ing, __ I'll keep re -

ash - es. _____
liv - ing. _____ } Where does love go, I don't know,

when it's all said and done? How could I be los - ing you __ for - ev - er af - ter all the

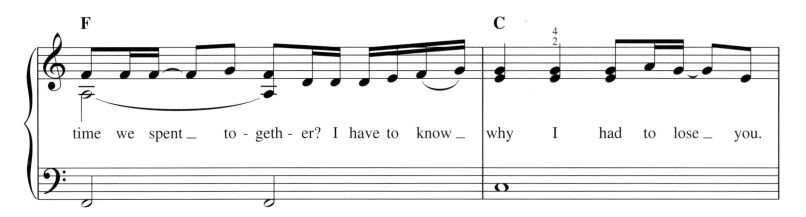

F ... **C**

time we spent ___ to - geth - er? I have to know ___ why I had to lose ___ you.

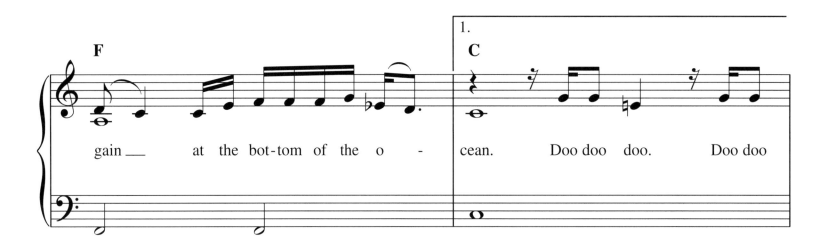

G ... **Bb**

Now you've just be-come like ev - 'ry- thing ___ I'll nev - er find a -

F ... **C**
1.

gain ___ at the bot-tom of the o - cean. Doo doo doo. Doo doo

G ... **Bb**

doo doo, doo doo doo doo doo doo doo. Da da da, ___ doo doo doo doo.

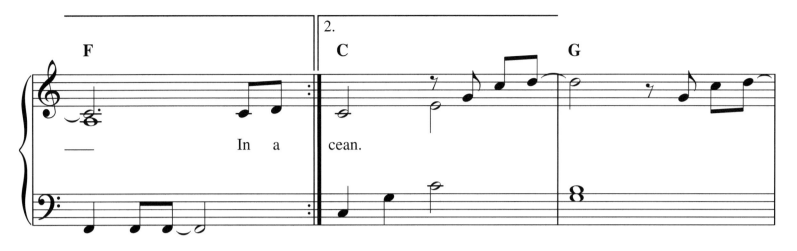

F | **C** | **G**

In a ... cean.

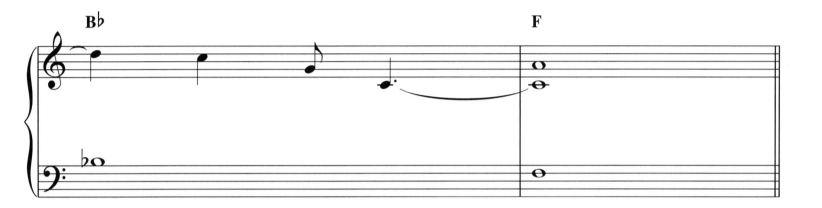

B♭ | **F**

C

You don't have to love me for me ___ to, ba - by, ev - er
I don't wan - na hold you if you ___ don't wan - na tell me you

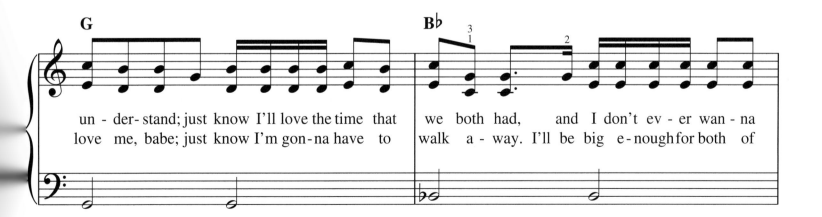

G | **B♭**

un - der - stand; just know I'll love the time that we both had, and I don't ev - er wan - na
love me, babe; just know I'm gon - na have to walk a - way. I'll be big e - nough for both of

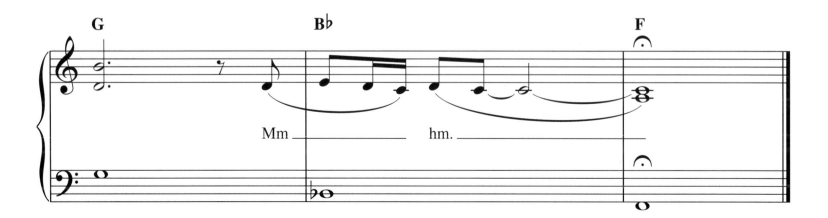

WAKE UP AMERICA

Words and Music by MILEY RAY CYRUS,
TIM JAMES, ANTONINA ARMATO
and AARON DUDLEY

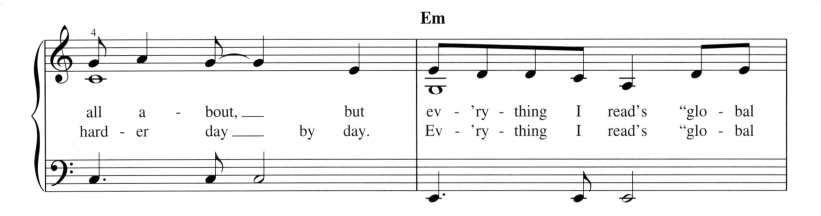

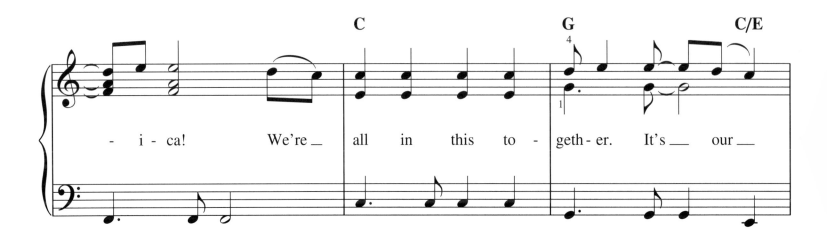

47

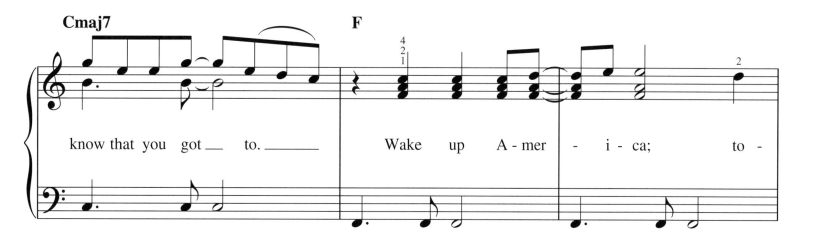

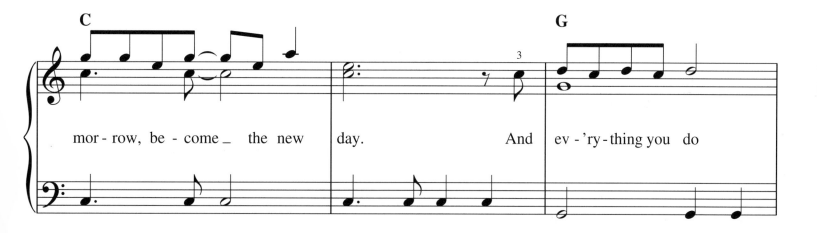

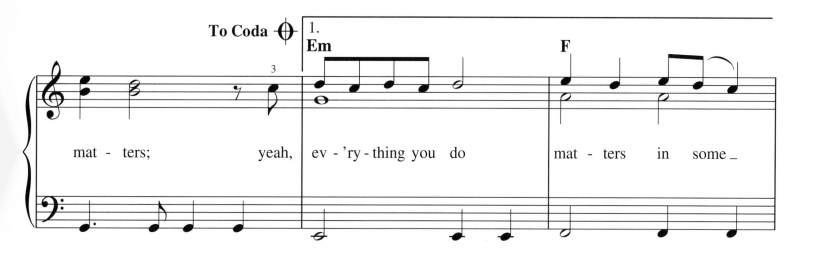

48

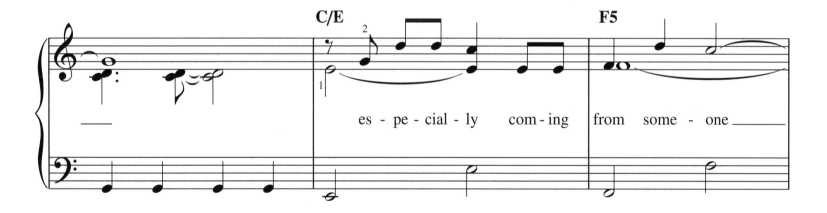

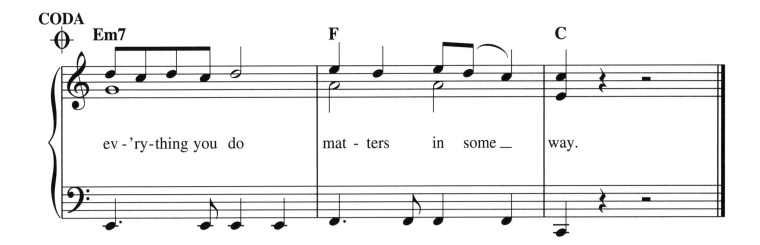

THESE FOUR WALLS

Words and Music by CHEYENNE KIMBALL,
SCOTT CUTLER and ANNE PREVEN

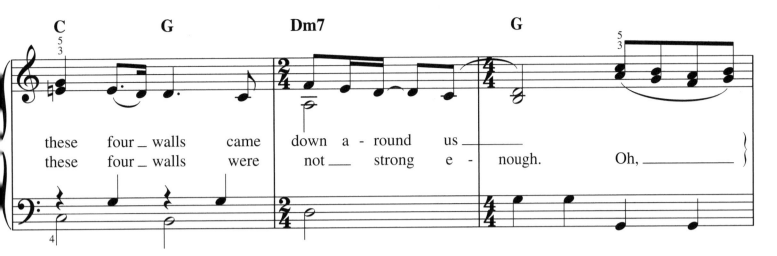

these four _ walls came
these four _ walls were

down a - round us _
not _ strong e - nough.

Oh, _

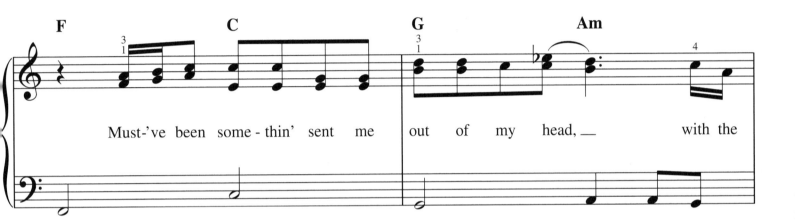

Must-'ve been some - thin' sent me

out of my head, _

with the

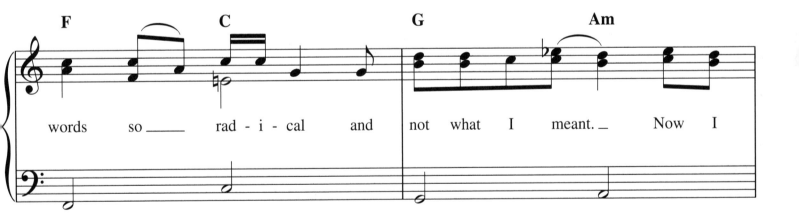

words so _ rad - i - cal and

not what I meant. _

Now I

wait for a break in the si - lence, 'cause it's

all that you left. _

just

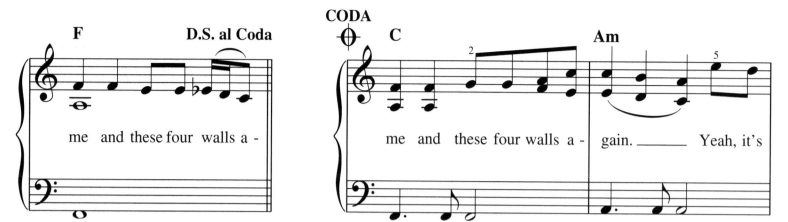

me and these four walls a-

me and these four walls a- gain. _____ Yeah, it's

dif - fi - cult _____ watch-ing us fade, know-ing it's all my fault, my _ mis-

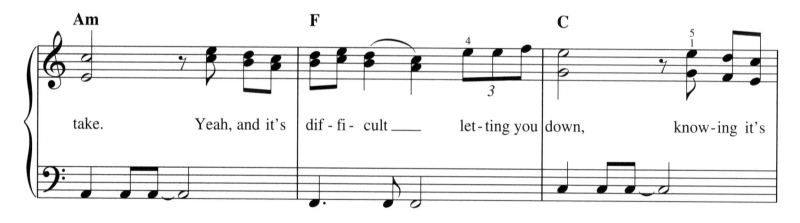

take. Yeah, and it's dif - fi - cult _____ let-ting you down, know-ing it's

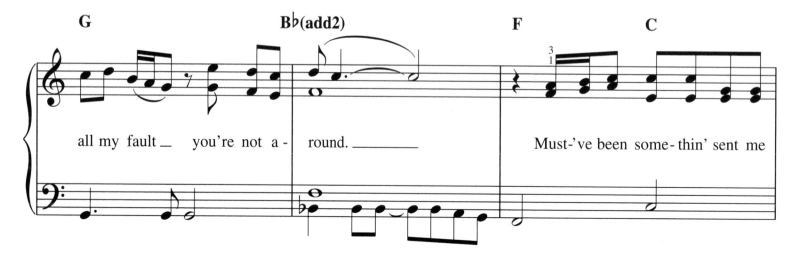

all my fault _ you're not a- round. _____ Must-'ve been some-thin' sent me

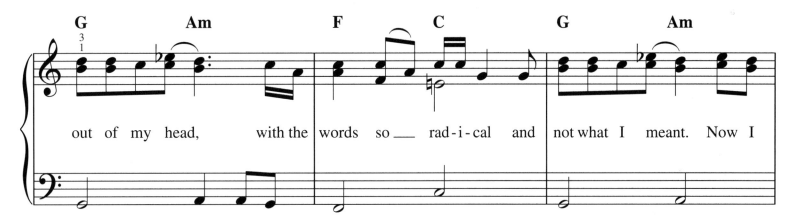

out of my head, with the words so ___ rad-i-cal and not what I meant. Now I

wait for a break in the si - lence, 'cause it's all that you left. ___ Just

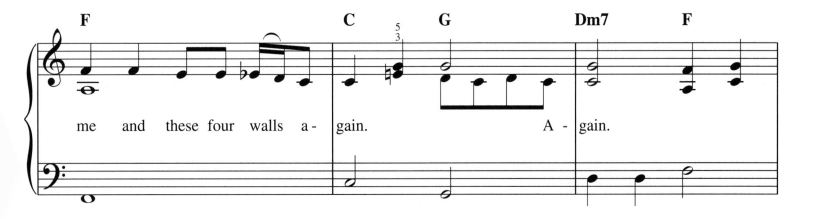

me and these four walls a - gain. A - gain.

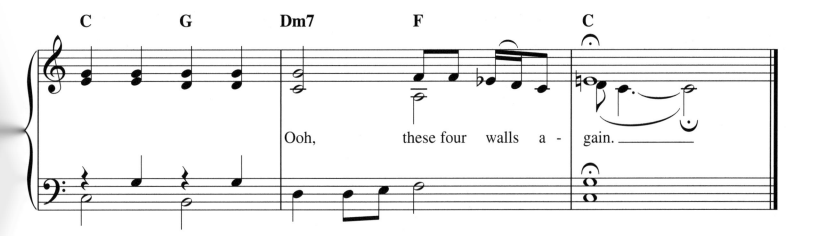

Ooh, these four walls a - gain. ___

SIMPLE SONG

Words and Music by JESSE LITTLETON
and JEFFREY STEELE

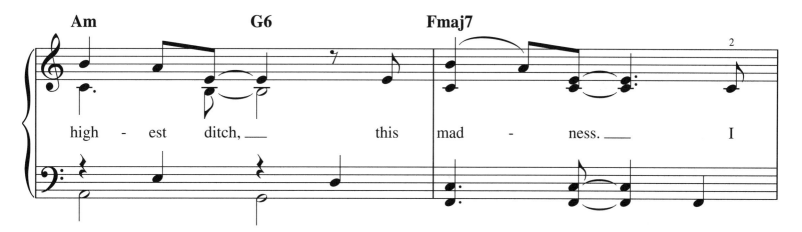

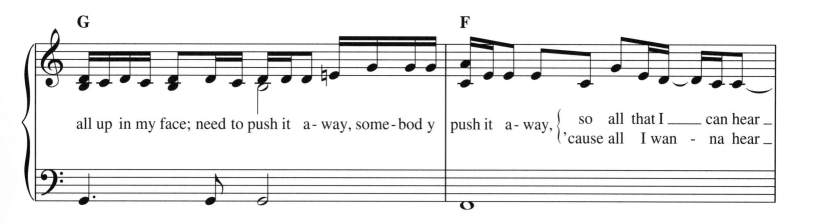

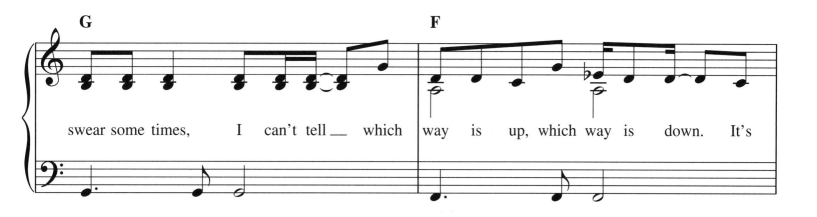

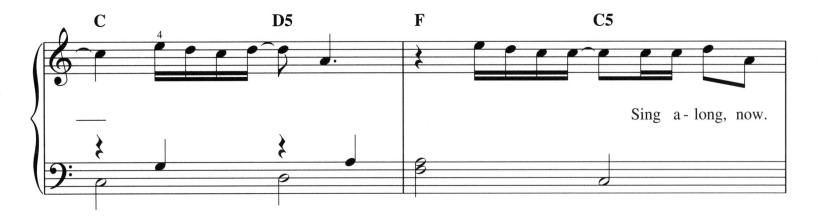

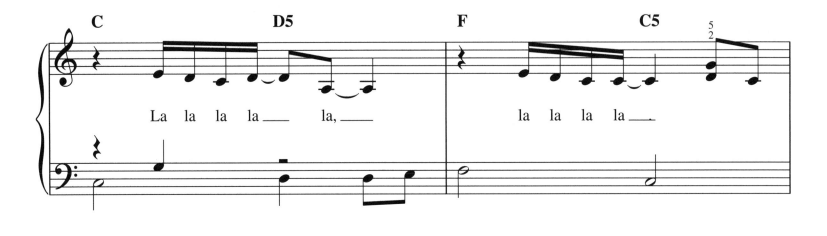

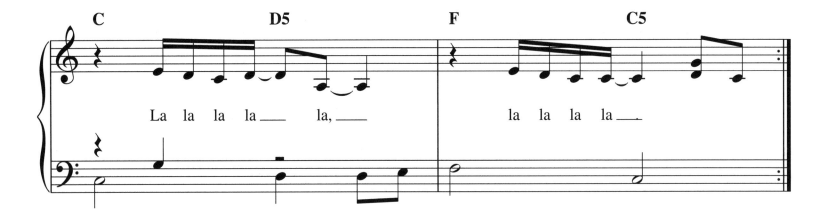

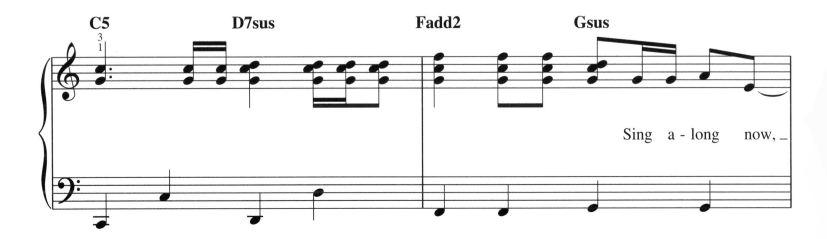

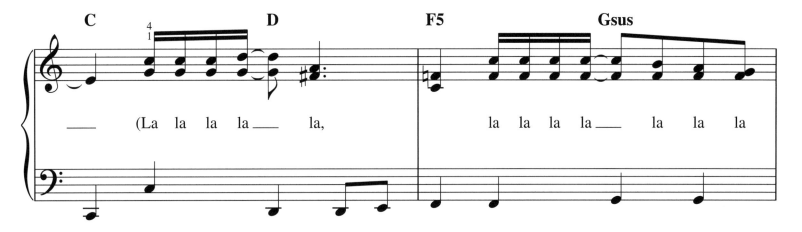

(La la la la___ la,   la la la la___ la la la

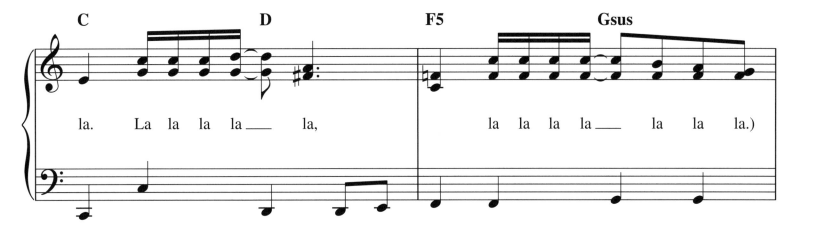

la. La la la la___ la,   la la la la___ la la la.)

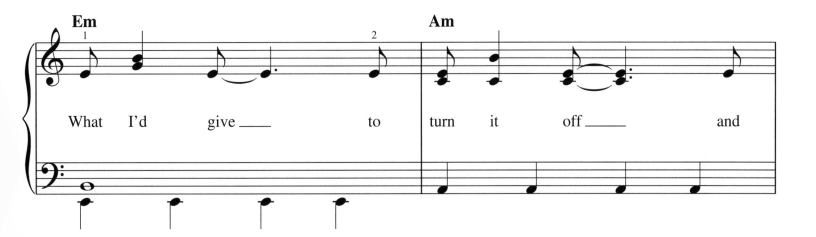

What I'd give ___ to   turn it off ___ and

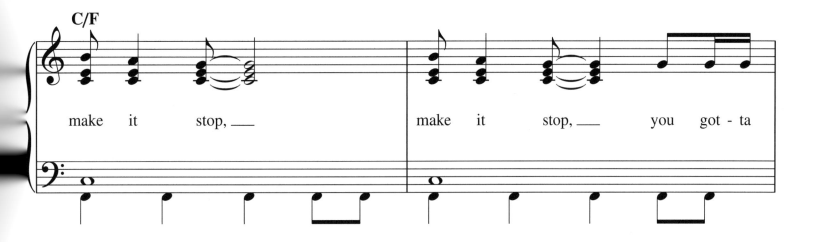

make it stop, ___   make it stop, ___ you got-ta

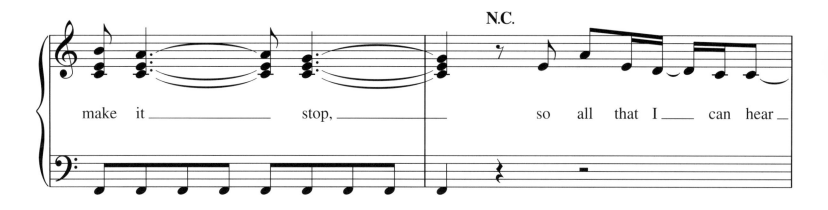

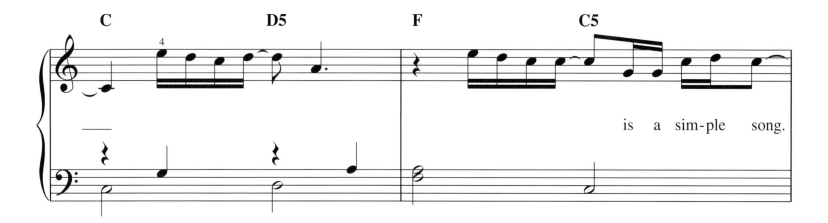

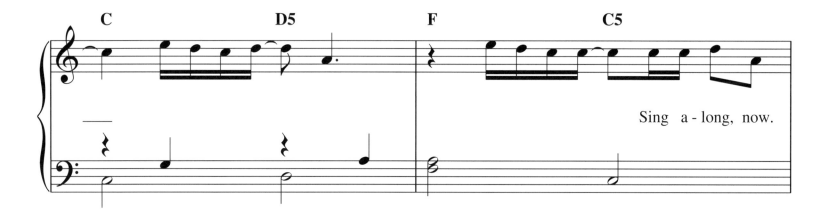

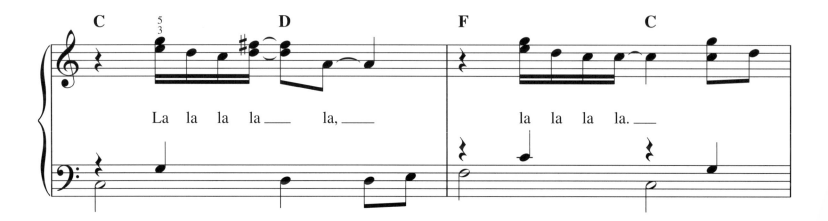

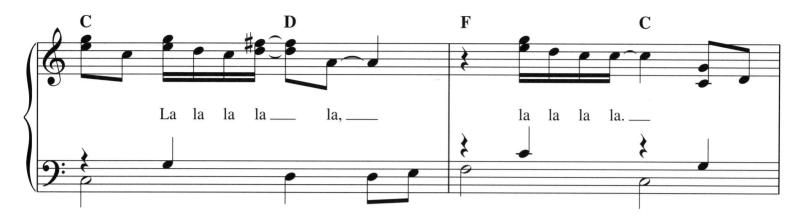

La la la la la, la la la la.

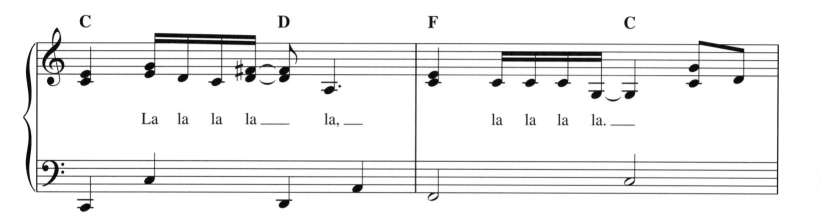

La la la la la, la la la la.

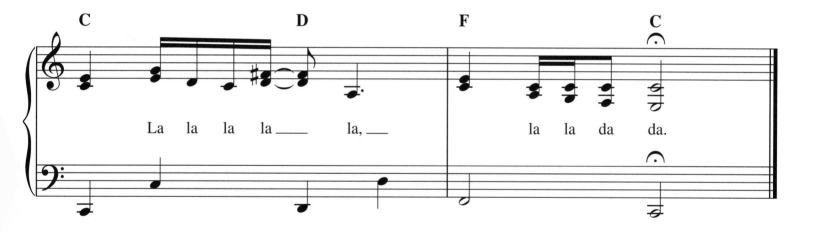

La la la la la, la la da da.

Additional Lyrics

Midday sun beating on the concrete, burning up my feet.
Too many cars on the street.
The noise, the red, the green makes me wanna scream.
Five o'clock now; it's bumper on bumper on bumper,
Horns honkin'; nobody's lookin', but ev'rybody's talkin'.
Just another day on this highway.

I swear sometimes...

GOODBYE

Words and Music by MILEY RAY CYRUS,
TIM JAMES and ANTONINA ARMATO

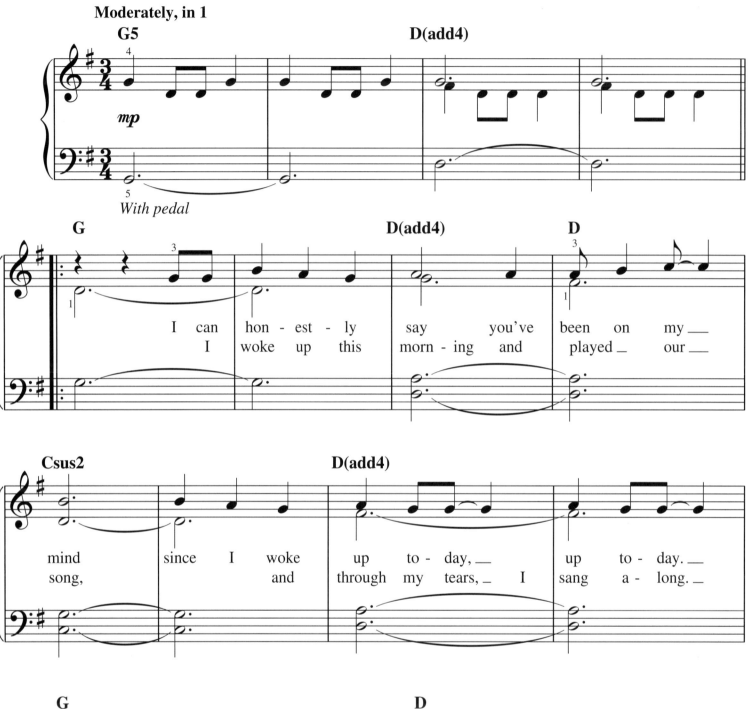

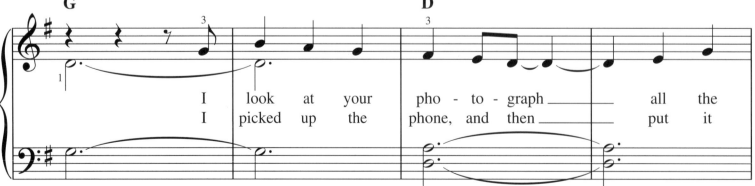

61

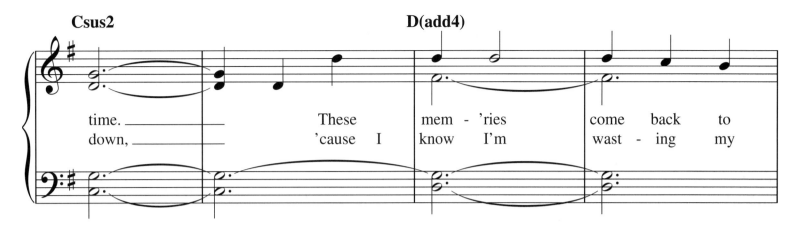

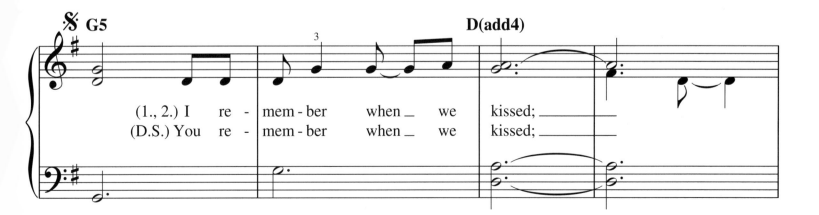

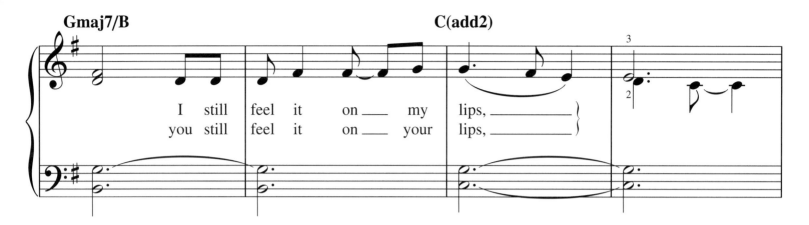

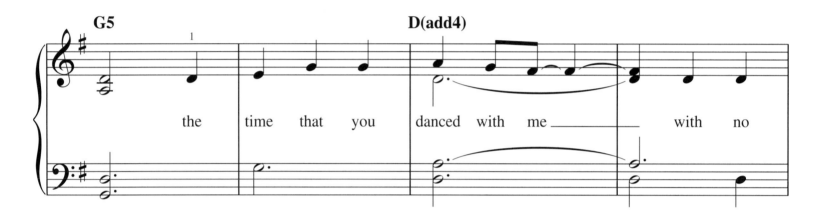

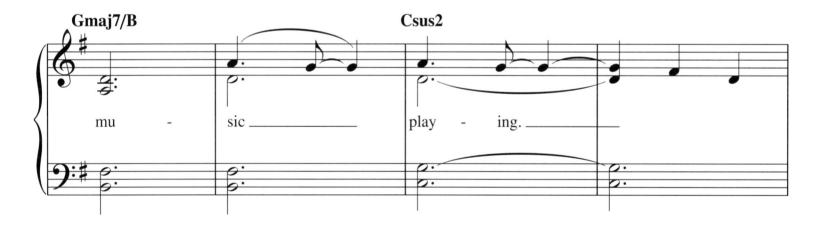

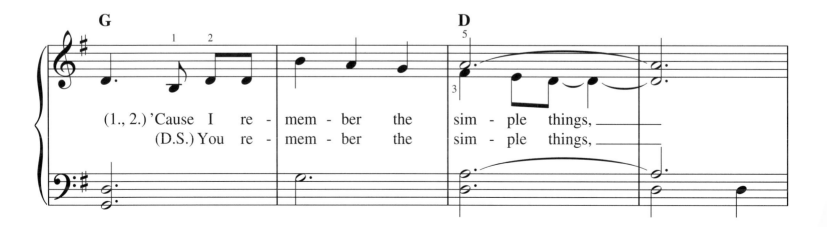

I _____ re - mem - ber till ___ I cry. _____ But the
we _____ talked till ___ we cried. _____ You

one thing I wish I'd for - get, _____ the
said that your big - gest re - gret, _____ the

To Coda ⊕

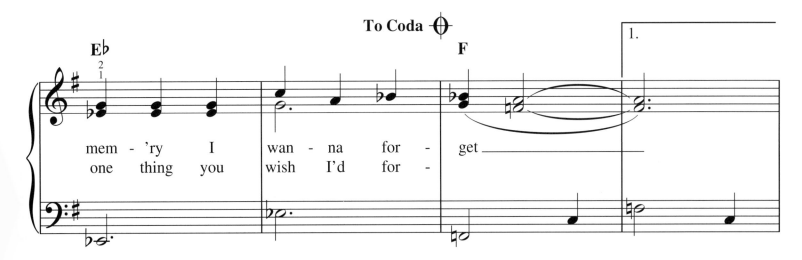

mem - 'ry I wan - na for - get _____
one thing you wish I'd for -

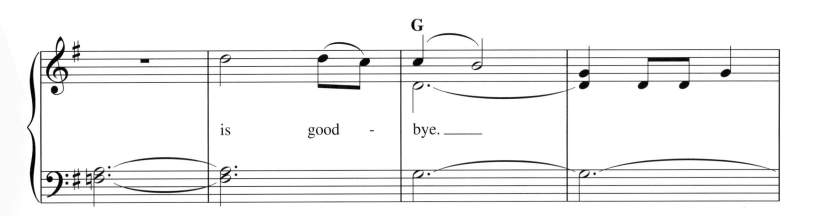

is good - bye. _____

64

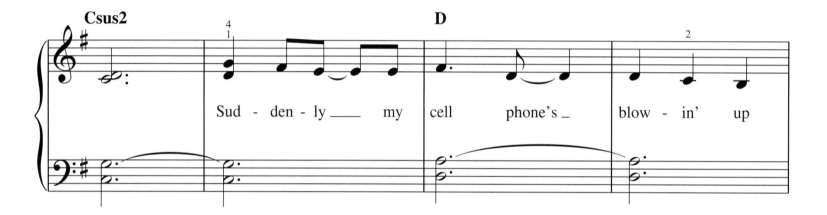

Sud - den - ly ___ my cell phone's ___ blow - in' up

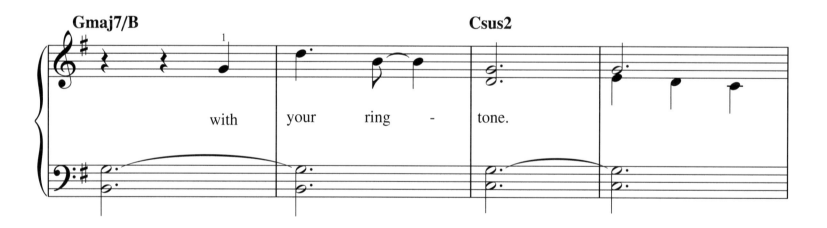

with your ring - tone.

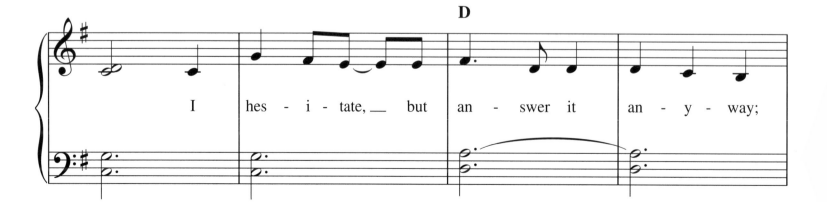

I hes - i - tate, ___ but an - swer it an - y - way;

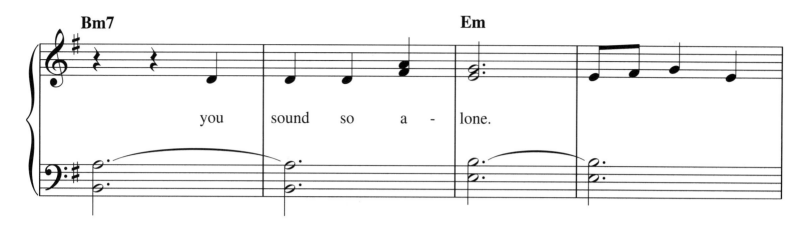

you sound so a - lone.

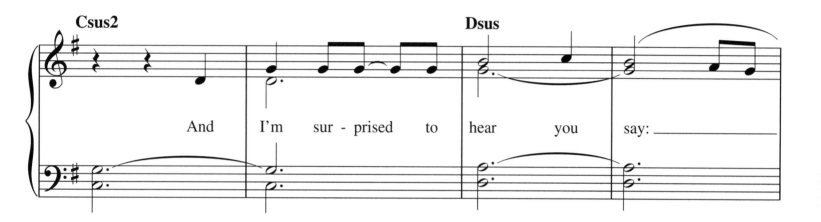

And I'm sur-prised to hear you say:

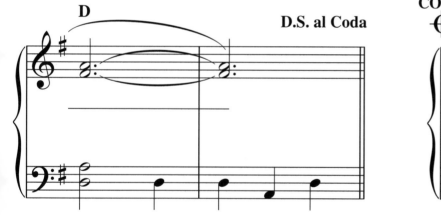

D.S. al Coda

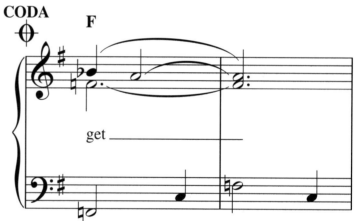

CODA

get

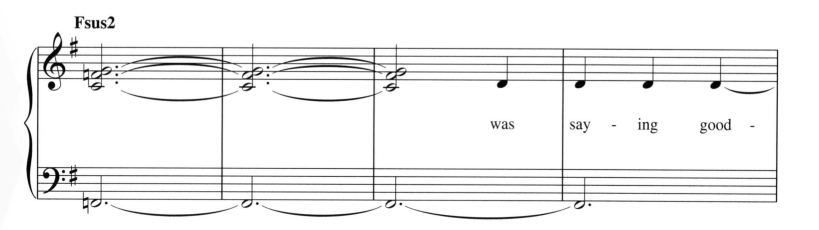

was say - ing good -

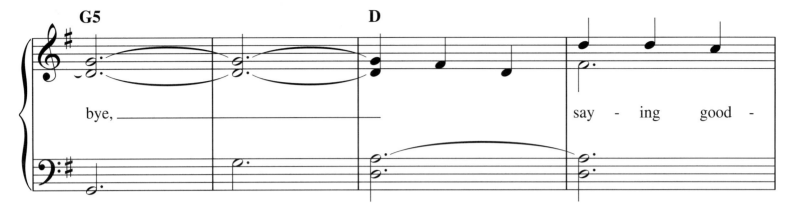

G5   **D**

bye, _____ say - ing good -

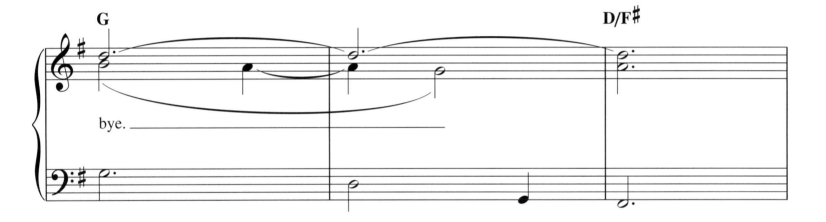

G   **D/F#**

bye. _____

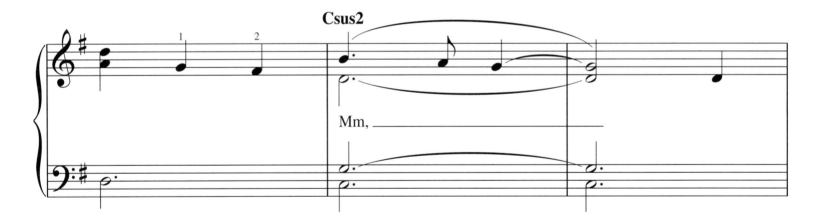

Csus2

Mm, _____

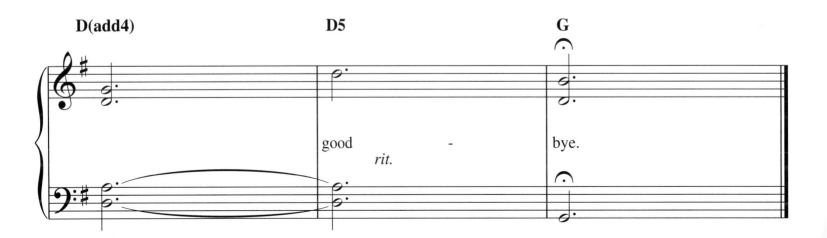

D(add4)   **D5**   **G**

good - bye.

rit.

SEE YOU AGAIN

Words and Music by MILEY RAY CYRUS,
TIM JAMES and ANTONINA ARMATO

Moderately fast

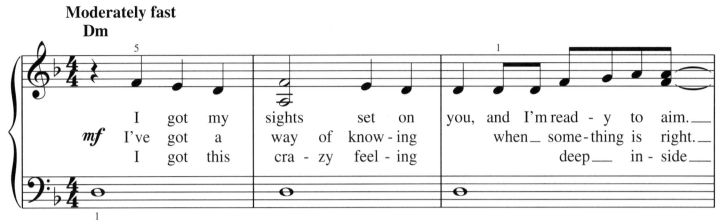

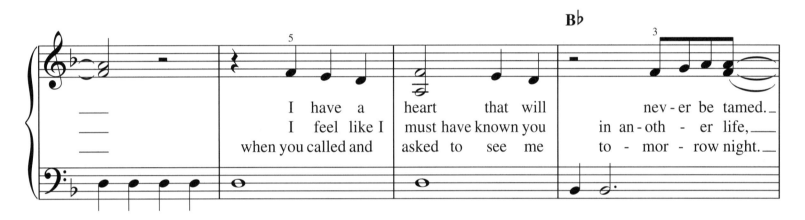

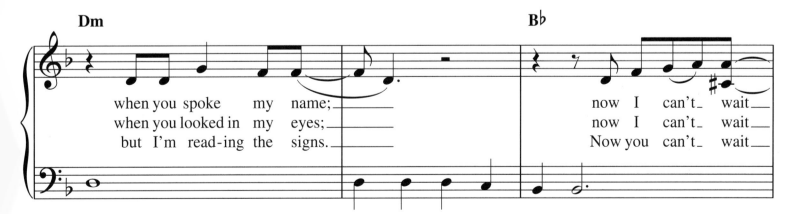

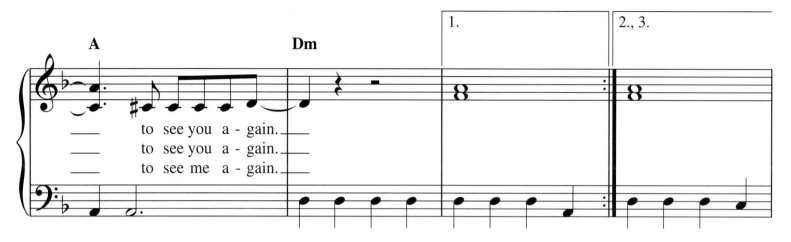

A   **Dm**   **1.**   **2., 3.**

_____ to see you a - gain. _____
_____ to see you a - gain. _____
_____ to see me a - gain. _____

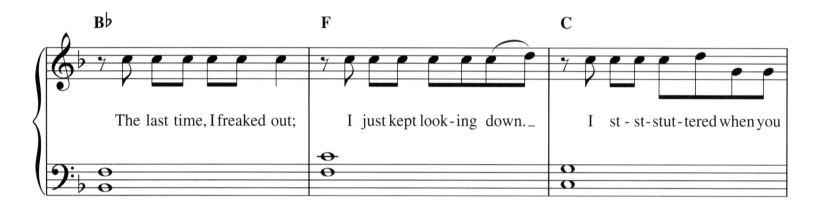

B♭   **F**   **C**

The last time, I freaked out;   I just kept look-ing down. _____   I st - st-stut-tered when you

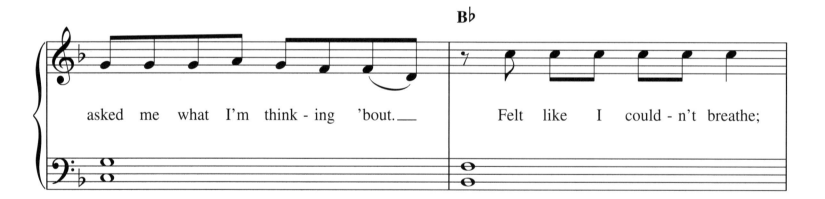

B♭

asked me what I'm think - ing 'bout. _____   Felt like I could - n't breathe;

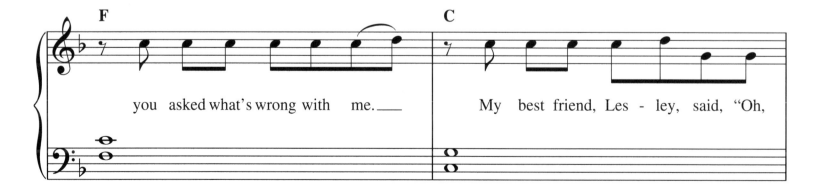

F   **C**

you asked what's wrong with me. _____   My best friend, Les - ley, said, "Oh,

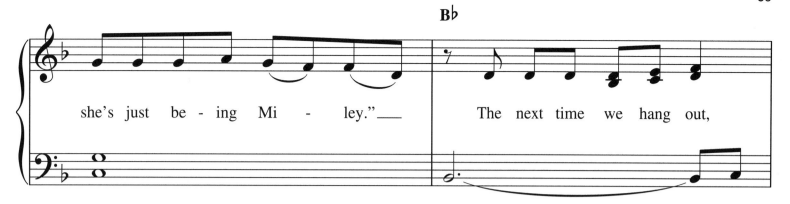

she's just be - ing Mi - ley." The next time we hang out,

I will re-deem my - self. My heart, it can't rest 'til then. Oh, whoa, whoa,

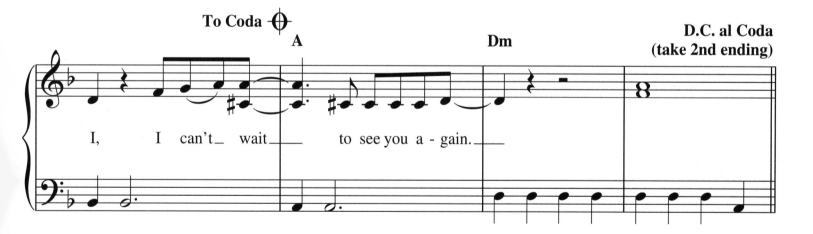

To Coda ⊕

D.C. al Coda
(take 2nd ending)

I, I can't wait to see you a - gain.

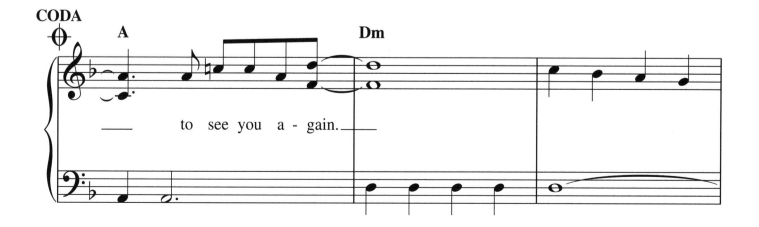

CODA
⊕

to see you a - gain.

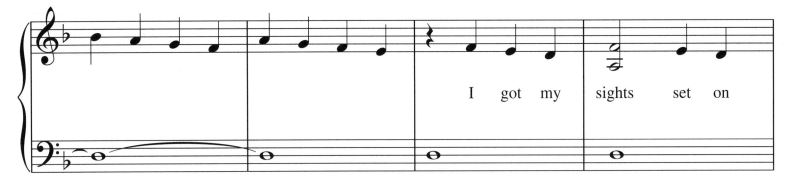

I got my sights set on

you, and I'm read-y to aim.___

B♭

The last time, I freaked out;

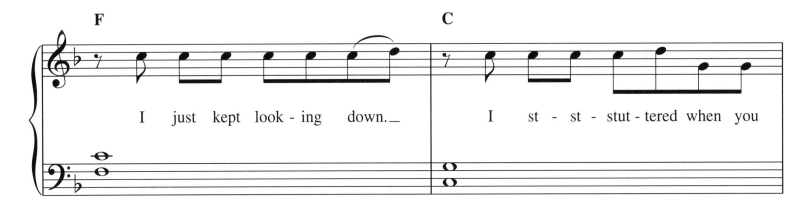

F

I just kept look-ing down.___

C

I st - st - stut-tered when you

asked me what I'm think-ing 'bout.___

B♭

Felt like I could-n't breathe;

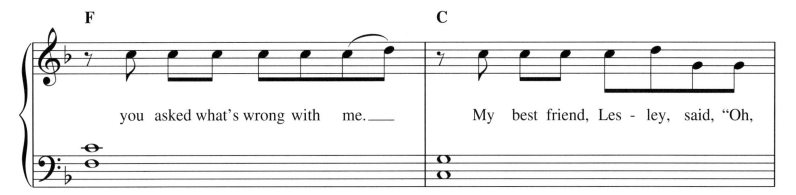

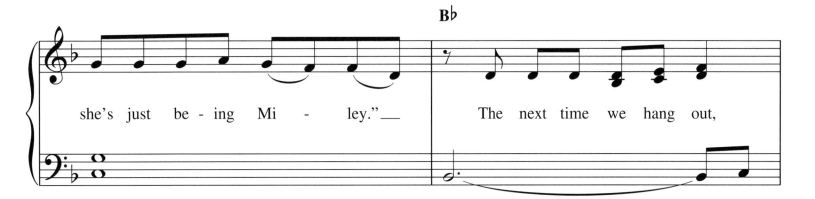

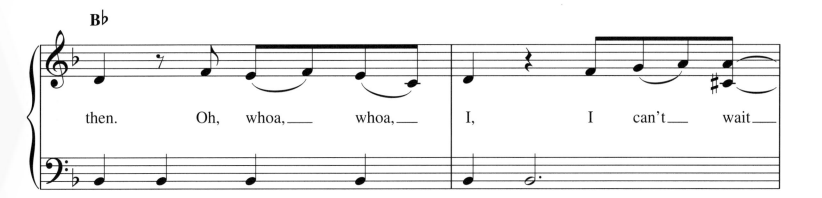

72

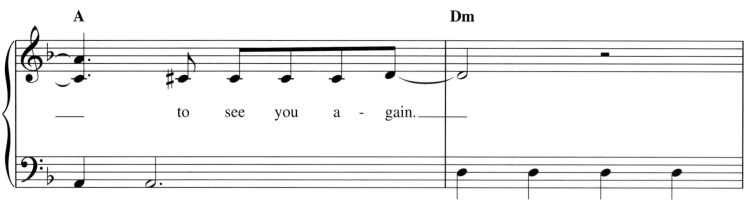

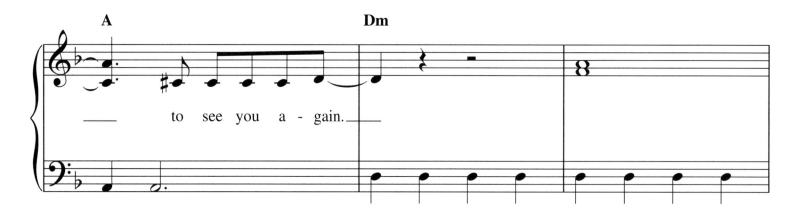

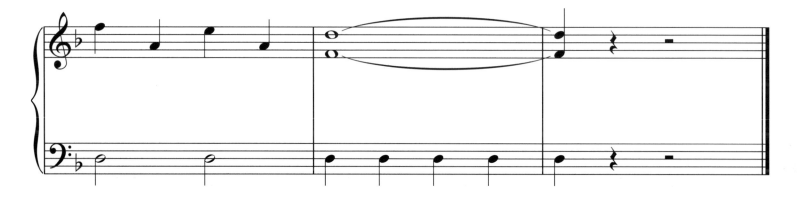